"Julie Hliboki is a healer, spiritual guide, a student of mystery, and a keen observer   and awe of being human. Her latest collection of poetry, images, and stories invite the reader to wade in where the water is deep, exploring how to be respectful of the currents of nature and graceful in the process of aging. She uses meditative suggestions to create a sense of spaciousness and stories to illustrate our shared human connection. In a culture where the gifts of aging often go unsung *Going to Essence: Aging into Wisdom with Intention and Grace* is refreshing, comforting, and wonderfully thoughtful."
—**Carrie Newcomer**, Songwriter and Poet, *Until Now* and *The Beautiful Not Yet*

"This beautiful book is a garland of jewels of wisdom and great kindness."
—**Roshi Joan Halifax**, PhD, author of *Standing at the Edge: Finding Freedom Where Fear and Courage Meet* and *Being With Dying: Cultivating Compassion and Fearlessness in the Presence of Death*

"*Going to Essence* is a beautiful collage of encounters that leaves you pondering upon multiple dimensions of existence. Read it slowly. This book may well become one of your treasured sources of intentional energy to return to periodically."
—**Shams B. Syed**, MD, Head Of Unit, Quality of Care, World Health Organization

"Julie Hliboki, with a grace and courage that is aspirational for many of us, provides a resource that engages mind, body, and spirit in places where the questions run deepest. This book is more than just a reflection companion; it holds us in the Light even as we journey into places that we do not seek but cannot avoid."
—**Trace Haythorn**, PhD, Executive Director/CEO, Association for Clinical Pastoral Education (ACPE)

"*Going to Essence* is a dance of grace and hope. The poems and photographs have a prophetic role. They are about being and becoming, encouraging reflection, and inspiring a deep understanding of what it is to be human. This is a book where we can see the passing places of life, feel and understand the essence of time, recognise the generosity of life, and sing with joy because we value ourselves and each other."
—**Liz Grant**, PhD, Professor of Global Health and Development, University of Edinburgh

"After reading a few of Julie's selections and reflecting on each Intention and Grace, I had a tingling sensation of calm, compassion, and renewal flowing throughout my body. My mind wandered to my grandparents and their Essence, Aging, and Wisdom, which I am so blessed to have known and loved. An often missing smile came to my face, and I was thankful."
—**Bruce Compton**, Senior Director, Global Health, Catholic Health Association of the United States

"In *Going to Essence*, Julie Hliboki invites us to breathe, laugh, and remember what we know to be true. This book is a gift."
—**Ashley M. Wilcox**, author of *The Women's Lectionary: Preaching the Women of the Bible throughout the Year*

"Too often our fast-paced lives rob us of the time required to keep ourselves centered and our intentions clear. This beautiful book can be a powerful resource as we seek to live our lives fully and at peace with who we are."
—**The Rev. George Handzo**, APBCC, HealthCare Chaplaincy Network

Breathing Light:
Accompanying Loss and Grief with Love and Gratitude

Bearing Witness:
Quilts and Stories Honoring Life in a Children's Hospital

Replenish:
Thirty-Three Openings to the Sacred

Cultivating Compassion in an Interfaith World:
99 Meditations to Embrace the Beloved

The Breath of God:
Thirty-Three Invitations to Embody Holy Wisdom

Compassion Meditation Cards:
An Interfaith Approach to Cultivating Compassion —
For You, for Others, and for the World!

GOING TO ESSENCE

Aging into Wisdom with Intention and Grace

JULIE HLIBOKI

PHOTOGRAPHY BY:

DAVID FOSTER, BRYAN P. SPERRY, CINDY ADDISS, JULIE HLIBOKI, AND DAVID ADDISS

TRANSILIENT PUBLISHING

For all of the Wise Elders
who graciously impart
their compassionate guidance,
may your voices and stories
continue to be heard.

GRATITUDE

Every element of creating a book is an act of love for me, part of my offering to the world. My intent and hope are to encourage self-awareness, inspire compassion, and further the realization of our interconnectedness, all with a dab of wisdom, humor, and grace. I know I've been "successful" when I receive a letter from a reader conveying how deeply they were moved in body, mind, or spirit by a poem which helped them no longer feel alone; or an email expressing how uplifted a reader felt after a poem or two accompanied them through their loved one's death; or a note letting me know that a reader has begun a contemplative practice of reading a poem each day and sitting with its message for inspiration. These comments make my heart sing with joy!

Each stage of producing this book is precious to me. Some of the most enjoyable aspects are the relationships that interweave to support its creation. These connections fill my heart with love and gratefulness, and keep me grounded in the journey when I feel uncertain or vulnerable. I offer deep gratitude to the following persons who helped make this book a reality:

- To the Wise Elders in my life who inspired many of these poems, thank you for your love, kindness, and generosity to me. I miss you so much.
- To Bryan, David, Cindy, and David for contributing your exquisite photography to accompany the poems, thank you for conveying your love of nature in images.
- To Barb, Mary Ann, and Cynthia who read drafts and offered thoughtful edits, thank you for your friendship and keen eye.
- To Patrick, designer extraordinaire, whose talents bring together the elements of the book so beautifully, thank you for being so enjoyable to work with.
- To each reader, thank you for entrusting me with your valuable time and open heart.

May all of you find peace, wisdom, and well-being as you age.

CONTENTS

Essence—
the most significant aspect of a person or thing

Aging—
a life process in which particular capacities arise with time

Wisdom—
knowledge that is gained through a lifetime of experiences

Intention—
what one determines to bring about in a particular way

Grace—
the quality of being compassionate to self and others

Over the past decade or so, I have had the good fortune to provide spiritual care and well-being programs in children's and adult hospitals, inpatient hospice units, home healthcare, and senior affordable independent-living communities. This work has helped me to witness what it means to be human—the ache and awe associated with living and dying.

I have held the hands of mothers as their child dies, applauded patients after successful bone marrow transplants, tended to teens who completed suicide, and rejoiced with centenarians celebrating their 100th birthday. I have prayed with families as goodbyes were expressed during final breaths, attended cancer treatments with those who had no family or friends, cheered on babies who left the neonatal intensive care unit healthy, and held Celebrations of Life for communities that had suddenly lost a dear friend.

While ushering in peace and comfort in countless traumatic situations, I have received more love and gratitude from "strangers" than I thought possible. It is difficult to express how this work has shaped me into the person I am, how it has grounded me in patience, compassion, and love. These experiences have helped me truly understand the human condition.

Being human means we will ache; we will suffer. We will find ourselves at times confused, lonely, in pain, grief-stricken, outraged, fearful, depressed, hopeless—the ache we all have felt in body, mind, and spirit. And being human means we will experience awe in the miracles we witness every day—wonder, gratitude, friendship, love, kindness, beauty, and compassion. As we age, we have an opportunity to move more deliberately toward awe even as our aches increase. We can move toward acceptance and gratitude and away from resistance and bitterness. We can move toward love and compassion and away from judgments and condemnation. We can move toward wholeness and grace even as age unravels our body and mind. It is our essence—our essential nature—to become wise from our lifetime of experiences.

During my work, I have witnessed incredible courage, strength, dignity, faith, love, and friendship in the face of impossible hardship, unbearable pain, and intense suffering. The people I have accompanied are stellar examples of what it means to cultivate wisdom as we age—not ever easy but exceedingly necessary for our spiritual, emotional, and mental health. Wisdom enhances our well-being no matter our physical condition.

Going to Essence: Aging into Wisdom with Intention and Grace offers a glimpse into some of my most precious encounters. The poems and stories I've written are seeded with morsels from conversations, observations, and prayers with those who have blessed me with their presence, wisdom, and love. I encourage you to read the entries aloud, particularly those written in first person. My hope is that you are able to imagine yourself within the universal essence of each poem and story.

I endeavor to cultivate wisdom as I age. Every morning I arise and begin my 60-minute contemplative practice—a combination of Buddhist meditation, Quaker Healing Light ceremony, Sufi prayers, and a lot of silent listening. At the end of each hour, I continue to sit in silence and wait until an intention becomes clear in my mind. This intention guides me throughout my day. I like having just one intention. This gives me permission to not have to juggle numerous intentions, which can often leave me feeling harried, self-judgmental, and lacking. I can manage the focus of one Spirit-led intention for the day. This leaves me feeling centered, purposeful, and resilient.

Most important, I find that my intention moves me toward grace for all those I encounter during the day. I am more forgiving, peaceful, flexible, and kind with family, friends, strangers, and myself. I have included with each poem and story an invitational "Intention and Grace" prompt that you can try throughout your day or select your own intention based on your response to what I've written.

May you embrace the aging process—allowing it to reveal your essence, to cultivate your inherent wisdom, and to help you live with intention and grace.

Julie Hliboki, February 2022

GOING TO ESSENCE
Aging into Wisdom with Intention and Grace

The Gazebo Girls

The Gazebo Girls meet every morning, rain or shine. Most arrive with mugs of steaming hot, strong coffee. Some have cigarettes. They sit in a circle, a gathering of friends, and share stories, struggles, and wisdom. Peals of laughter permeate the conversation. Like the sounds of church bells, the laughter alerts everyone within hearing distance that there is more to the present moment than we realize. Amid the worries, the rushing, the waiting, the uncertainty, and the pain . . . love, joy, and light abound.

I stop by to check in. I am welcomed warmly. They shift their seating on shared wooden benches so that all have plenty of room in the crowded, intimate space. This morning they talk about their excellent treasures acquired during the latest thrift store outing. A few are wearing their finds, and proudly announce with glee the great deal they scored. Others nod approvingly and relate to the fun of making scarce dollars stretch.

The conversation shifts from raucous laughter to a subdued tone. A regular Gazebo Girl is absent this morning. She is in the hospital, yet again, for her serious health condition. Several discuss her circumstances and how they can best support her with visits, pet sitting, healthy food. Others sit quiet with bowed heads. I imagine all are reflecting on their own experiences of pain, suffering, and hospitalizations.

Voices drift into shared silence, weighted by the enormity of possibly losing another friend. I ask if they would like to hold this dear one in the Light with me. The Gazebo Girls enthusiastically nod their heads and we all join hands in prayer. We begin holding our loved one in the Light and collectively create a powerful force. I sit in awe of the fierce love and determination pouring forth from our small, outdoor congregation.

I can imagine, on a clear night, such an intentional energy beam of Light might be visible from the moon.

INTENTION AND GRACE

May I celebrate friendship today

One Hundred

The room is filled
with statues
of the Virgin Mary,
four or five deep
to a bookshelf,
desktop, and dresser.

Perhaps one hundred
are present
along with crosses,
images of Jesus,
and dozens of rosaries
hanging in every
nook and cranny.

"My mother loves
shopping at thrift stores,
as you may be able to tell,"
her daughter relays
with a giggle.

As I enter the room,
I sense a holy presence,
one of love, grace, and peace.
Mom is sleeping deeply,
her beautiful gray hair
combed and arranged
around her tranquil face.

Her body is covered
in a prayer shawl
handmade by a friend.
I can sense that she
is close to end-of-life.

We hold a blessing ceremony,
my version of Anointing the Sick,
and invite mom to release
into the Beloved's arms.
She draws her last breath
among one hundred witnesses,
everyone smiling
and welcoming her home.

INTENTION AND GRACE

May I sense today the Holy Presence

How Great Thou Art

From down the hallway
I hear gospel lullabies
Sung strongly and clear

His voice booms with praise
How great thou art, oh Lord, Yes!
Send your love to me

My footsteps quicken
I knock on his door, inquire
He beckons me come

Our souls fill with light
It is good to see you, friend
We share all we have

INTENTION AND GRACE

May I sing praise and honor life today

This Moment

Gratitude is
the essential ingredient
for happiness and peace.
We must accept
and be thankful
for what we have
rather than focus
on what we might
be lacking.

Don't bring the past
into the present,
nor worry
about tomorrow.
The most important moment
is this moment
you are living
right now.

We cannot change the past,
nor control the future,
but we can focus every day
on becoming
a better person.

It is our obligation
as a human being
to give love,
to help others,
to develop inner peace.
Only a deep, committed love
can save the world.

INTENTION AND GRACE

May I be present today

Honor Me

I knock on Nadia's door. From inside I hear a thick Lebanese accent yell, "Come in!" I open the door and say, "Hi Nadia, it's Chaplain Julie." "Sweetheart!" she yells, "It is so good to see you. Come in. Come in and sit down."

I enter Nadia's simple, tastefully decorated efficiency apartment. To the left is a dining room table filled with international foods–modjoor dates, blanched almonds, baklava, oranges, and babaganoush. Her table is a constant offering of abundance, overflowing with nutrition for the body, heart, and soul. I walk to her couch and sit next to her recliner.

I inquire how she is today. Nadia lets me know that the cancer has spread. She says this matter-of-factly as she peers into my eyes. She reminds me that she does not want chemo or radiation, that this is her third bout with cancer, and that she is ready to answer God's call to bring her home. My heart aches. I am not prepared to lose her. I long for more time with her, to get to know her better. As if reading my mind, she begins to tell me a story.

Nadia is from Lebanon. She immigrated to the U.S. alone with her five young children. She learned English and then taught Arabic at the local university for much of her career. She raised her five children and is so proud of them. Her story is filled with rich details of love, heartache, survival, courage, and dignity.

She takes my hand and, with tears in her eyes, reassures me that God will look after her children when she is gone. I can see that she is in a lot of pain, physically and emotionally. I ask her what she needs and she just shakes her head. We sit in silence, holding hands, she with her eyes closed, me watching her face.

Suddenly, she brightens and smiles broadly.

"Yes," she says, "I do need something. I need you to take with you the dates and almonds on the table."

"Oh, Nadia," I reply, "Thank you, but no. Those are yours, I cannot take them."

Nadia laughs and says, "HONOR ME!" I am startled. She repeats, "You must HONOR ME by taking this food! This is what we do in my country. We feed those we love. Please take this food!" I am at a loss for words. How can I say no?

I leave with a container filled with dates and almonds. To this day, I cannot eat a date without remembering Nadia. I am grateful. Perhaps she knew.

INTENTION AND GRACE

May I share the love of those that I carry in my heart today

Invitation

Emotional triggers are gifts that reveal
Where I am in need of healing

INTENTION AND GRACE

May I experience today the invitation
of unusual gifts

Best Friends

We've cared for each other
for the past 20 years.
We've been best friends
through sickness and health.
I know she is dying
but I will be lost without her.
Isn't there something you can do?

INTENTION AND GRACE

May I tend today to my
heart-felt losses

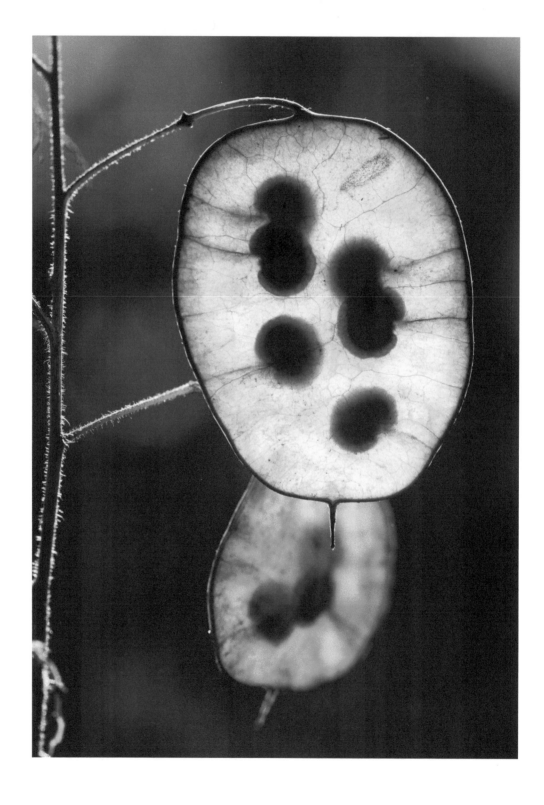

Wisdom

I am aware of a Wisdom
Greater than the finite me
That speaks to me and guides me
When I take the time to listen

This is my inner teacher
Perhaps *God*, but I prefer *Holy Wisdom*
Or *Sacred Light*
Or perhaps simply *Spirit*—mine, yours, all

This Wisdom arises in the prevailing moment
It resonates Love and Truth and Acceptance
Buddhist meditation moves me closer
Practice cuts through my ego

I am supported, enlivened, animated
I am brought back to my core being
I am reminded of who I am
Courage, strength, dignity

This Wisdom doesn't fix
It guides, moment-by-moment,
Breath-by-breath
I am becoming

Cultivating patience and self-compassion
Abiding with curiosity and humor
Releasing judgment and shame
I have a way to go

And Wisdom walks with me

INTENTION AND GRACE

May I listen today to my inner Light

Instigator

I've learned over the years
that things will come and go,
but a smile is eternal.
A smile can shift
your entire outlook on life.
I color my hair electric pink.
I like to instigate smiles.

INTENTION AND GRACE

May I offer a smile today to
those I meet

Doubt Has No Home

Thin as a willow
Frail as a whisper
Soft as pale smoke

I am sitting now
I'll be standing soon
Just wait and see

Sharp as a sabre
Certain as daybreak
Doubt has no home

INTENTION AND GRACE

May I encourage strength today

Ask

I ask for what I want.

I may not get it
but I can still ask for it.

If my request is rejected
so be it.

We all are responsible
for our own behavior,
me included.

I can rejoice in the asking.

INTENTION AND GRACE

May I ask for what I need today

Pebbles

The most important bit of wisdom I've learned in my seventy-five years is compassion, compassion for everyone. You never know what someone has been through, what drives them to make the decisions they make or behave in a certain way.

I actually appreciate people who are difficult. They are like pebbles in my shoe. My response to them requires a deeper level of awareness, something more than an autopilot answer. A pebble reminds me of their pain, their suffering, their need for my compassion. A pebble also humbles me. A pebble reminds me that I am human, that I too suffer, that I make mistakes, and that I need self-compassion.

Much of the time I am pebble-free, living life with abundant joy—but I always welcome pebbles.

INTENTION AND GRACE

May I offer compassion today to others and myself

Indelible Imprint

"Chaplain Julie," she says with a broken heart, "please pray for me. I've just lost my son."

This is the fourth such request I've received from residents in the past thirty days. The death of a child at any age is terribly painful, even if the loss is an adult who has lived a full life, even when the death is expected. And when it is unexpected, the pain is unbearable.

I wrap my arms around her as she sobs on my shoulder. She tells me it was an accident at work … that he slipped and fell … hit his head … a concussion … an emergency room … a hospital … no recovery. I can only imagine how wrenching this must be.

We say a prayer together, asking for strength to get through this difficult period. The tears flow mournfully until the sobbing slowly subsides. Through bleary eyes she looks directly into mine and says with determination, "I am grateful for the time I had with him. He is with God now. Thank you, Chaplain Julie. Please continue to hold us in your prayers." Her request leaves an indelible imprint on my heart.

INTENTION AND GRACE

May I remember today that everyone is carrying something painful

Healing

Some wounds
cannot heal
from the outside
but must heal
from the inside out—
deep cuts, burns,
nearly every wound
that penetrates the flesh.

The ache in my heart
over his lack of love
or connection to me
is a deep wound.
I have been hoping,
working at,
open to,
healing that wound
from the outside.
This is not going to work,
cannot happen.

He could help
the wound heal
by applying
the ointment of love,
but that has not happened.
It will not happen.
I must stop hoping
for what is not
and concentrate
on healing
from the inside out.

I started this process today,
imagining the wound healing,
just like a deep cut
might begin to heal.
I apply the ointment,
the good intentions,
visualize the mending process,
the body's amazing ability
to heal itself.

I can protect
the vulnerable skin
from being
torn open again,
and not put myself
in harm's way
to be wounded again.
I can trust myself,
my body,
to heal itself.

Breath aids the healing.
Each in-breath provides
spaciousness

and focused healing energy.
Each out-breath provides
a clearing and opening
for more healing in-breath.

The wound heals from within,
not from the outside.
This is true for everyone.

We can help create conditions
for healing from the inside,
but we cannot
do the actual healing
from the outside
for someone else,
try as we might.

We can provide
advice and comfort
for how to heal,
but each individual
does his or her own healing.
We can offer wisdom, support,
and love,
   which is a lot
   but, ultimately,
   the healing comes
   from within.

INTENTION AND GRACE

May I attend to that which
needs healing today

Attachment Theory

Bowen got it right
Thriving requires healthy attachment
Love, connection, compassion, presence
These are key ingredients to being fully alive
I'm sure of it

Most of us lacked healthy childhood attachment
We now need to be that for each other
Love, connection, compassion, presence
These are key ingredients to being fully alive
I practice cultivating them every day

INTENTION AND GRACE

May I reach out today to those I love

Biscotti

At one with her recliner
In the same way
She is at one with her cancer

At 95, she says, it's time to go
But until then, she will dine on
Homemade ice cream and biscotti

No need to nudge or foil death

INTENTION AND GRACE

May I take my time today

Faith in Truth

I waited patiently for You, my Beloved.
   You reached for me
     and listened to the call of my heart.
You offered me Your hand
     to lift me out of the quagmire,
and set me solidly upon my feet,
     making my steps sure and complete.
You helped me find my voice,
     to speak my truth.
With grace and compassion,
     I put my trust in Your Ways.

INTENTION AND GRACE

May I speak my truth today
with strength

Spirit's Prayer

Holy Creator and Sustainer
Whose love enlivens all beings
Let us rejoice in our relation to all

Whose sacred presence is everywhere
Whose essence permeates every thing
On earth and throughout the galaxies

Give us this breath, this present moment
And relinquish our past and future fears
So that we may open our eyes and value all beings

And lead us on a path of truth, honor, and justice
That delivers us from ignorance, greed, and suffering

For this is our true nature
The compassionate way
The embodiment of your Spirit

Amen

INTENTION AND GRACE

May I walk with Spirit today

Resilience

He spent his life as destruction
Hurting himself, hurting others
Pain arising and dispensed from his own wounds

And yet they rally around him
Family pouring out care, compassion, grace
Wanting only his comfort during the final weeks

Where does their resilience come from
The ability to look past all of the hurt and sorrow
Caring for the one who was incapable of caring

I inquire
He's family, they say…
But do not mistake our benevolence as forgiveness

INTENTION AND GRACE

May I care today for those I
struggle with

Desire

I want you to reach out to me
when I arise in the morning
and ask me to stay.
I want you to reassure me
that moving slowly, taking our time,
will be worth our while.
I want you to adore my body,
kiss my toes, stroke my hair,
and relish every part of me.

I want you to listen to me
as though what I said could
alter the world.
I want you to speak to me
with every word wrapped
in love and respect and gratitude.
I want you to respect me
as if I could move mountains
and create galaxies.

I want you to hold me
as though at any moment
I might disappear.
I want you to love me
unconditionally, without expectation,
false reverence, or criticism.
I want you to see me
for who I am, separate from you,
yet also a part of you.

I want you to encourage me
to explore, to push boundaries, to
initiate new wonders.
I want you to hold the space
where I can melt into nothingness,
and arise cracked open, raw and vulnerable.
I want you to stand with me
in my enraptured joy
and breathe deeply and knowingly.

I am in wonder
that this might be.

INTENTION AND GRACE

May I express my desires clearly today

Refuge

I find shelter in the arms of You, my Beloved,
    knowing that even Your shadow provides refuge.
I declare to You that I have found inner strength,
    and my soul rests in tranquility.
I need not fear losing myself,
    or being caught by anxiety's snare.
I am held securely in courage and dignity,
    and under these wings I find refuge,
    for I now know that I am never alone.
I fear not the unease of my unquiet mind,
    or the angst that can fill my days,
    or the worry that can stalk in darkness,
    or the fret that squanders a moment.
For I called to You, and You answered me.
    You are with me in my troubled thoughts,
    You liberate me and hold me close.
Filled with love and grace I sense Your presence,
    which reveals my path of recovery.

INTENTION AND GRACE

May I find refuge today

Survival

For months, maybe years
Weekly, or perhaps daily
It seemed that way, anyway…
   unbearable
I tried to get it out.

All the external criticism
The messages of unworthiness
The cycles of ridicule, punishment, shame
The pain of abuse
An incursion on my essence, my existence…
   crazy-making
I tried to get it out.

I purged, a dry bulimic
For there was nothing consumed
There was only that which invaded me
From the outside, from others
From those who were to protect me…
   untenable
I tried to get it out.

I gagged and released
Felt relief momentarily
The physicality of my body
All of my senses alert
Awakened to me, to being present
Even in this wrenching state.

Trying to get it out
I didn't know that's what it was
I thought I was sick, or had issues
But mostly I didn't think
Just felt the liberation that something had exited
Something I could flush away
A stand-in for the intolerable.

Now I know…
Trying to get it out
Was trying to save my life.

INTENTION AND GRACE

May I hold gently today that which
kept me alive

We Are One

I am grateful to You, my Beloved,
    and all that is within me
    is blessed with appreciation and gratitude.
My soul delights in the world's interconnectedness,
    and remembers the love we can cultivate for each other.
Let us respect our differences,
    let us nurture healthy relationships,
    let us restore broken hearts,
    all with steadfast love and mercy.

INTENTION AND GRACE

May I recognize interconnectedness
today

Silver Thread

My twin sister has died
I cannot go on without her
I miss her too much

She is here with you
Have you spoken to her
She is available to you at any time

How, how do I do this
How do I find her
How do I connect

Follow the Silver Thread
It links your heart to her heart
And her heart to your heart

Close your eyes
Imagine a Silver Thread
It begins in your heart

The Silver Thread grows like a beanstalk
Twisting and twirling
Avoiding any barrier

The Silver Thread moves swiftly
Toward your loved one
Your sister's heart

Allow the Silver Thread to connect
To begin the flow of information
Like two cans on the ends of a string

Feel her love
Send her your love
She is always available to you

INTENTION AND GRACE

May I connect today to those I miss

She Is All I Have

Covered in tattoos
He cares for his grandmother
With such tenderness

He spoon-feeds her life
One morsel, one memory, love
Her eyes say thank you

She is all I have
A bond forged in strength, courage
Wisdom, dignity

Total dependence
Yet emanating power
They sit hand-in-hand

Her eyes close for now
Her breathing deepens slowly
A bodily peace

She is all I have
Pray, let her live one more day
We bow our heads, plead

INTENTION AND GRACE

May I give thanks today for those I love

Do No Harm

He asked…
why bother
with self-examination
why not just,
oh, well,
here I go again,
that's just
who I am?

I hear…
why not
there I go
again
inflicting
my pain
on others
creating
unnecessary
suffering
all because

I am unwilling
to do my own
inner work
toward greater
self-awareness.

why indeed?
(deep breath)

I respond…
we do our work
to do no harm.

INTENTION AND GRACE

May I do no harm today

Age Is Only a Number

The heart is forever young
Age is only a number

Peace comes when we accept
That the body will decay
But until that final point
We must help others

Freedom comes from trusting that
If I do not have food today
I may have food tomorrow
And, I can share whatever I do have
To help someone else
Helping others
And giving thanks to God everyday
Makes me a better person

This is where I find happiness
Not outside myself
But within myself
By living a life of giving

It keeps me youthful
My heart forever young

INTENTION AND GRACE

May I express my happiness today
through giving

Vespers

Played with God's passion
Gnarled hands sweep weathered keys
Piano chords hum

A glance from her eye
Choir stands with grace and poise
Books open to praise

Ten voices in song
Harmonies beautifully blend
Vespers comes alive

INTENTION AND GRACE

May I come alive today

Unshackled

She asked:
how do you know
if your memories are true?

Ugh…after a lifetime
on the receiving end
of gaslighting,
I bristle
but create space
for the innocence
within the question.

I ask myself:
how do I know
if my memories are true?

Photos, scars,
medical records…
experiences lodged
within my DNA,
trauma embedded
in my body,
PTSD disorientation.
I exhale deeply.

My memories
have to be true,
right?

I feel destabilized
holding the question,
yet notice a thin tendril
of freedom
winding its way
into my consciousness
as I play with
what "true" might mean.

Is the memory true?
Undoubtedly my experience
is true for me.

Perhaps the query
requires expanding…
What is my story
surrounding the memory?

How does my perception
of the other's intention
influence the memory?
Accurate but incomplete?

With renewed curiosity
I ask the question:
Are my memories true?

Perhaps accurate
but unquestioningly incomplete.
Freedom arises
as I unshackle fixed images.
My memories call out for
liberation, a letting go
of impressions too rigid,
including "truth."

INTENTION AND GRACE

May I hold my memories lightly today

Shine

Listen sweetheart,
always enjoy
each day
as it could be
your last.

If you wake up
feeling dreary,
remind yourself
you don't want
to miss out
on enjoying
this day.

As long as
you rise,
you might
as well shine.

INTENTION AND GRACE

May I enjoy today

Nine AM? Really?

"Really, Chaplain Julie? Do you really need to start Breath Meditation at 9:00 am? Do you have any idea what it takes for me to get ready in the morning?" Leila asks only half rhetorically. She is the first resident to show up for my new class, Morning Breath Meditation. I have planned an hour devoted to relaxation of the body and mind. Instructions are simple; follow the breath. Inhale spaciousness and ease, exhale into relaxation. I'm very excited to share it, yet Leila's questions have popped my "I've got this" bubble.

I look at Leila, 91 years old, hunched shoulders, thick eyeglasses, nearly blind. Her graceful gray hair is swept back with a headband that matches her comfortable, neat clothes. I am amazed and honored that she has come to my meditation class. Little do I know how much I will learn from her over the next three years.

"Actually Leila, I'm so sorry, but I have no idea what it takes for you to get ready in the morning," I reply. "Well" she says with a smile, "let me tell you!" Over the next few minutes, as we wait for more participants to arrive, Leila describes a daily two-hour process that begins upon awakening. Given her ailments, back issues, and chronic pain, I learn that it takes enormous effort just to get out of bed and get dressed. I learn about the timing of various medications, which ones need to be taken before meals, with meals, after meals. I learn about the effort it takes to make a meal, to clean up, to read the paper with headlamp magnifying glasses. All of this accomplished oh-so-slowly. I hadn't a clue.

As she shares her morning schedule, Leila begins laughing. Joy emanates from every part of her. I struggle to understand how a body so weary and hurting can laugh so abundantly. Then Leila exclaims with great exuberance, "But I'm alive!! I am here another day! And I get to learn breath meditation!"

By this time, about a dozen residents have filled the small circle of chairs I've set up in the library. "Welcome to Breath Meditation," I say invitingly. One of the residents says, "I'm happy to be here, but 9:00 am, really?"

We now gather at noon.

INTENTION AND GRACE

May I laugh and share my joy today

Many Colors

We were raised in the hills of Tennessee
By people of many colors—African, European, Indigenous
My daddy said race didn't matter

He said it was about what you do with your life
Separation is everywhere—African, European, Indigenous
Do what is right, live by example, honor all

He said it's what's in someone's heart that counts
So I loved everybody—African, European, Indigenous
Our lives were intertwined, interdependent, interracial

I always felt safe and interconnected
They looked out for me—African, European, Indigenous
How do we return to this?

INTENTION AND GRACE

May I honor all today

In My Eighties

I advocate for seniors
with government officials and lawmakers
because I am passionate about promoting our needs.

So many politicians depend on our votes
but they do not listen to our cries.

It's too easy to push older people aside,
to believe that we have nothing to offer.

They don't understand how much wisdom
arises from toil and despair, and overcoming hardships
with courage and dignity.

We seniors must use our voices to be heard.

Young people may appreciate that they too
will be seniors at some point, and that this will happen
sooner than they realize.

Our advocacy work will benefit the future for all generations.

INTENTION AND GRACE

May I advocate today for the
most vulnerable

Labyrinth

Befriending the grief
Carried deep in my bones
My heart releases compassion

INTENTION AND GRACE

May I befriend my grief today

Dragon Breath

No, not the type
when someone
blasts you with garlic
or forgot to brush this morning.
This is the Dragon Breath
that begins deep in your bones—
the fire of injustice,
rage, fear, pain.

Past raw spots brought to life,
heat in the body,
a large, steaming opening
at the center of the sternum,
like a ring of fire
surrounding the sun—
red, pulsing, diffuse,
but concentrated in the core.

Blindsided by the lies,
confused by the crazy-making,
pain from the loss
of something precious,
rage and fear pour through
words that still haunt.

Heat exhaled forcefully
through the mouth,
alternately inhaling oxygen
through the nose.
Haaaaaaaaaa—
released fire
until the throat is hoarse.
Dragon Breath is incinerating
every injustice in its path.

Wisdom arises.
This visual of activated fury
feels so personal and threatening,
so anger provoking,
a raw spot of past pain and rage
and violation
like someone is inside
still hurting me.

The Dragon breathes
into and out of the fear,
connects to all those
currently experiencing
unfairness, injury, rage, suffering.

It begins to soften, feel soothed,
not feel so isolated and painful.

My relationship to those
who have wronged me arises
filled with sadness and grief.
The Dragon begins to ache
but is no longer raging.
Compassion abounds.

I hold these suffering beings
in the Healing Light
knowing our path
is out of my hands,
but our interconnectedness
is forever.

The Dragon Breath settles
into a gentle pulse
harmonized
with my beating heart.

INTENTION AND GRACE

May I breathe through today what
seems impossible

Good Deeds

Whenever you do a good deed for someone, the positive ripples continue to bless others. For example, about sixty years ago in my home country I remember working with a young girl who had a very difficult life. She was abandoned as a child, suffered many hardships, and was in terrible shape. She stole money from the store where I worked, and when caught, threatened to take her own life.

I took her home with me. I cared for her and nurtured her, and eventually convinced her of her worthiness, to not commit suicide. She promised me she would not do that. Years later I learned through friends that she was happily married with children. Imagine all of the blessings that arose from her choice to live, all the people she was able to love and nurture. This made me incredibly happy.

What a wonderful gift to know the results of my helping this young girl during troubled times. You never really know where your good deeds will lead. You just need to keep doing them.

INTENTION AND GRACE

May I practice good deeds today

Breathe

At any time
I can breathe through
my immediate, momentary
reality.

Window to the Soul

Vibrant eyes
reveal the wisdom
of a thousand ancestors.
Death is simply
the next adventure.

INTENTION AND GRACE

May I embark today on a
new adventure

Passageway

Angry at everyone
Her wrath spares no one
All are to blame
Such is her passageway of grief

INTENTION AND GRACE

May I be gentle today with those
who are grieving

Freedom

Rescuing behavior,
overextending,
pulls me off balance,
outside of myself.
I lose touch with my core.

The opposite of overextension
is not deflation or defeat.
It is centeredness,
in touch with my essence,
acting from a place of solidity.

From this locus,
I am able to recognize
the difference between
rescuing and responding,
inviting movement.

Often, there is nothing for me to fix.
I can experience my feelings
and calmly move on.
I don't need to rescue anyone or flee.
This is freedom.

INTENTION AND GRACE

May I respond today rather
than rescue

Daughters as Midwives

Peaceful,
floating in water
like amniotic fluid,
liquid that cradles, comforts, caresses.

She has entered the passageway.

The end of now,
the beginning of birthing next.

You are her midwives.

Hands of comfort, love, and touch,
bathe her in light,
encourage her to gently make her way
into the next realm.

INTENTION AND GRACE

May I embrace today both endings
and beginnings

Hands of Light

In my mind's eye,
I carry the image
of God creating the world.
His arms are outstretched
over the earth,
His hands forming all of creation.
This is the image I pray,
not the cross,
but the birthing of life into being.

I close my eyes,
connect to this source,
and feel God's presence.
I imagine light coming from His hands,
as a beacon, a searchlight,
scanning the darkness.
He is always searching for us,
looking for me.
The light touches everyone
who is praying in that moment
and illuminates the path to God.

INTENTION AND GRACE

May I be a beacon of light today

But I'm Ready

I told
God
I am ready.
Why
am I still
here?
        Perhaps
        you still
        have more
        love
        to give.
Oh!
Then I
may be here
for a
long time.
        Yup.

INTENTION AND GRACE

May I rest today in Spirit's timing

I Am Not Alone

Whenever I am suffering,
I know that I am not alone.
Many people throughout the world
are experiencing comparable suffering
at any given time.

I close my eyes and imagine
all of my kindred spirits
calling out for relief—
through prayer, through community,
through our collective humanity.

I imagine my love and compassion
pouring forth and touching each person,
soothing each cry.

With each exhale I offer relief and peace.
With each inhale I accept peace and relief.
Breath-by-breath I connect to universal compassion,
which eases the suffering of all,
including mine.

INTENTION AND GRACE

May I offer peace and relief today to
those who are suffering

Wow

Her smile dazzles
So good to meet you, chaplain
We are glad you're here

My history is tough
But I am a survivor
And look at me now

Grace, vitality
Beautifully crafted by God
Style, poise, charm . . . wow

Miracles

Ninety-nine percent of life is composed
of seemingly uneventful moments,
yet each moment
contains an ocean of miracles.

When you find yourself struggling
to find meaning or purpose
I invite you to notice,
in that moment,
which ocean droplet, which miracle,
is asking to be revealed.

Share that miracle with someone
and become part of the river
of meaning, purpose,
and miraculous moments.

INTENTION AND GRACE

May I notice life's miracles today

Loving-kindness Practice*

Loving-kindness, or Metta, meditation helps clarify that there is no separation between you and your loved one. We are all connected and belong to a grand oneness. Comprehending this is particularly important at the end of life. When a loved one dies, the connection between you and your loved one persists.

By practicing loving-kindness, we learn to expand the capacity of our hearts to open toward greater self-awareness and to nurture this oneness. We become better able to acknowledge who we are and learn to fully accept ourselves, integrating all aspects of our experiences—those we consider both positive and negative—into our whole being. Appreciating ourselves allows us to embrace others and to recognize all goodness and difficulties as part of the richness of life. Acceptance fosters our sense of connection.

Through loving-kindness we become increasingly forgiving, forging our capacity to bestow compassion. Forgiveness encourages us to shift our focus from ourselves back to a state of mind that supports the oneness of all. Compassion enables us to bear witness to suffering and to have empathy for all beings. Compassionate acts begin by sensing from within what it must be like to undergo someone else's experience.

Metta practice begins with cultivating loving-kindness for oneself, then loving-kindness toward loved ones, friends, community, strangers, those we struggle with, and, finally, all sentient beings. The Metta practice can be profoundly moving as a method to cultivate forgiveness, compassion, and love, and to sense connection. I have found that this meditation aligns my heart, mind, and soul into a unified, beneficent force. I am able to cultivate the resources required to energetically hold others and me in a state of wellbeing. This leads me to an actively engaged connection with the Beloved in all. It encourages a dynamic commitment both to those I'm with and to the greater world.

These two contemplative practices were included in the book Breathing Light: Accompanying Loss and Grief with Love and Gratitude. *Given their wide appeal and helpfulness, I offer them again.*

Reciting the Metta Prayers

Begin by sitting and making any slight adjustments to your posture so that you are comfortable. Start with the first prayer, which offers loving-kindness to yourself. (If you find that it is too difficult to begin with yourself, start with the second prayer, which offers loving-kindness to a loved one.) After each offered prayer, have a moment of silence.

May I be happy.

May I be well.

May I be safe.

May I be peaceful and at ease.

May you be happy.

May you be well.

May you be safe.

May you be peaceful and at ease.

As you continue the meditation, you can bring to mind other loved ones, friends, neighbors, people with whom you struggle, and finally all beings.

Tonglen Meditation at End of Life

The Tonglen meditation teaches us to have compassion for ourselves and for others. It is often easy to feel kindness toward those we love and cherish, especially if we are feeling happy and content ourselves. However, it can be very difficult to feel open and loving toward those we struggle with, fear, or experience as painful. To care about all people who are suffering, we need to embrace our discomfort rather than run from it. By opening our heart, releasing our own tensions, and feeling the discomfort, we can connect with the suffering of that person and our own suffering and awaken compassion for all.

The Tonglen practice teaches us to breathe in another's pain to create spaciousness for them, and to breathe out whatever would bring them relief and happiness. For example, if a loved one is dying, you, your family, your friends, and the dying person may all be suffering. As you inhale, imagine embracing all of that suffering, trusting your body will transform the pain into love. As you exhale, visualize sending healing, relaxing light and happiness to those in need. Tonglen can be done for those who are ill, those who are dying or have just died, or for those that are in pain of any kind. You may wish to include Tonglen in a formal meditation or practice it in the moment whenever you encounter suffering. The meditation can be envisioned for any number of beneficiaries, even the entire world.

Instructions

Tonglen in the moment—inhale pain, exhale relief and happiness.

Tonglen as meditation:

- First, rest your mind in stillness, and open yourself to receive spaciousness and clarity.
- Second, tune into physical sensations. Breathe in a feeling of hot, dark, and heavy and breathe out a feeling of cool, bright, and light.
- Third, work with any painful situation that is real to you and may be creating an obstacle. Inhale the pain and exhale liberation.
- Finally, enlarge the taking in of suffering and sending out of relief and happiness beyond yourself—to include your loved ones, friends, difficult people, and all beings.

Over time, your ability to be compassionate and your resiliency for holding suffering will expand and strengthen.

David Foster's award-winning, healing art nature photographs have been widely exhibited, and grace the walls of many healing environments as well as private and public collections. For more information, visit: *www.davidfosterimages.net.*

After a busy and fulfilling career in public service, **Bryan P. Sperry** returned to photography for the pleasure of looking more slowly and closely at the beauty around us. For more information, visit: *www.bpsperryphotography.com.*

Cindy Addiss, a high school special education teacher, loves capturing the beauty of the mountains and wilderness when on hiking trips with her husband Don.

Julie Hliboki enjoys photographing the mystical and spiritual aspects of nature, particularly those elements that inspire her to laugh aloud in delight. In these moments of joy, Julie is once again reminded of Spirit's true essence. For more information, visit: *www.JulieHliboki.com.*

David Addiss, a global health physician, recently relocated to Santa Fe, New Mexico. He finds the natural beauty of the area so compelling that a day rarely goes by without recording at least one exquisite moment with a photograph.

David Foster (DF)
Bryan P. Sperry (BPS)
Cindy Addiss (CA)
Julie Hliboki (JH)
David Addiss (DA)

Breathing Light: Accompanying Loss and Grief with Love and Gratitude

"In *Breathing Light*, Julie Hliboki has written yet another spiritually uplifting and artistically compelling book. Her meditations create a compassionate space in which we can embrace and honor the grief we experience as we accompany a loved one who is departing this life. She draws on wisdom from several spiritual traditions that offer solace and inspiration, and her words are perfectly paired with David Foster's wondrous nature photographs. Those images draw us in, inviting us to both lose and find ourselves in the beauty of creation. All who are caring for people as they return to the mystery from which they came will find a comforting companion in this beautiful book."
—**Parker J. Palmer**, author of *On the Brink of Everything: Grace, Gravity, and Getting Old*, *Let Your Life Speak*, and *Healing the Heart of Democracy*

"Care responders to those who are suffering or saying goodbye are often undernourished. Dr. Hliboki has produced a companion for that journey. The gathered wisdom and guiding thoughts help us to center on the beauty of relaxing our breath and capturing sacred moments. As mindfulness and other meditative practices account for routine health interventions alongside allopathic responses, Hliboki reminds us of the spiritual source of their power. This beautiful book will serve as an internal reference that soothes the soul so that another soul can be revered."
—**George Henry Grant**, MDiv, PhD, Executive Director, Spiritual Health at Emory Healthcare

"*Breathing Light* invites the reader into moments where suffering and pain is the threshold between this life and the Great Mystery beyond. Drawing on her experience as a chaplain and the wisdom of multiple faith traditions, Julie Hliboki demonstrates how these liminal moments are filled with vulnerability and opportunity for the patient and the caregiver. These moments can also be occasions where small kindnesses and attentiveness create sacred space grounded in compassion and care. The gifts of presence and accompaniment are great treasures for those who suffer and grieve. Combining story, art, and meditative exercises, *Breathing Light* offers an opportunity for exploration of one's own thinking about end of life transitions. In the process, it provides an inspiring resource for those who undertake this important ministry of caring."
—**Jay W. Marshall**, Dean, Earlham School of Religion

"Two thoughts recurred as I read Julie Hliboki's new book, *Breathing Light*. First, science has promised and delivered extraordinary improvements in health in the past century. It has taught far less on how to deal with death. Hliboki shares her experiences in easing the transition. Second, I once asked Dame Cicely Saunders, founder of St. Christopher's Hospice in 1967, the beginning of a worldwide movement, "What is the most important thing I should tell my family?" Her reply was, "Tell them they do not need to be with you when you die, but you do want closure with them in advance." Hliboki provides lessons on reaching closure."
—**Bill Foege**, Professor Emeritus, Emory University

Cultivating Compassion in an Interfaith World: 99 Meditations to Embrace the Beloved

"Religions do not have a strong reputation for creating compassionate or inclusive people—despite the clear teachings of their founders. We often emphasize belief systems instead of practices that actually change our hearts, minds and behavior. In this excellent and much needed book, *Cultivating Compassion in an Interfaith World* will help bridge this gap."
—**Fr. Richard Rohr**, O.F.M., Center for Action and Contemplation, author of *The Naked Now* and *Everything Belongs*

"The major premise of this book is simple: Compassion is essential for both personal and our collective well-being and happiness. Using meditation as the particular instrument of personal transformation, Hliboki integrates the wisdom of Eastern and Western religious traditions as she guides us through a process for deepening our capacity for compassion. In doing so she draws attention to the essential ingredients for a transformation of consciousness—finding our center; addressing our illusions; realizing our inter-connectedness with all being; and experiencing the divine essence that flows through our relationships with self, others and nature. This contemplative consciousness is the life force of a compassion that has the power to transform the human condition. Realizing it answers any question or doubt about our true purpose in life."
—**Robert G. Toth**, Past Executive Director, Merton Institute for Contemplative Living

"This is a beautiful, simple and open-hearted guide to contemplative practice. It contains much practical wisdom and will provide real support and encouragement to those seeking to live with greater compassion."
—**Douglas E. Christie**, PhD, Loyola Marymount University, author of *The Word in the Desert* and *The Blue Sapphire of the Mind*

"A wonderful comparison of the shared roots across religious traditions that lifts out the centrality of compassion. In concrete and inviting ways, *Cultivating Compassion in an Interfaith World* illustrates respect for each tradition while engaging the reader with creative suggestions to develop the practice of compassion within and across our traditions—a brilliant contribution to all of us concerned with finding ways to deepen our wells of kindness and build bridges across our many divides."
—**John Paul Lederach**, PhD, Professor of International Peacebuilding, Kroc Institute, University of Notre Dame, author of *The Moral Imagination: The Art and Soul of Building Peace*

"*Cultivating Compassion in an Interfaith World* captures the essence of compassion from different spiritual traditions showing us how common love is amongst all peoples. In spite of this, many people find it hard to practice compassion in their daily lives to others and to themselves. Hliboki's book presents practical contemplative spiritual exercises that can be easily taught to clinicians and others needing to integrate compassion into our own lives and helping them recognize the sacred in all we do. I strongly recommend this book to anyone searching for the sacred within and especially to those in the healing professions."
—**Christina M. Puchalski**, MD, Director, George Washington Institute for Spirituality and Health

"Hliboki has been blessed with a very precious spirituality, and she is, once again, moved to share it with us in a work that enriches the heart, mind, and soul. It is our prayer that God continues to bless her, and that she continues to publish these blessings."
—**Imam Plemon T. El-Amin**, Chair, Interfaith Community Initiative, Atlanta

"Like a prism of light, *Cultivating Compassion in an Interfaith World* refracts the pure light of the Beloved into a gorgeous spectrum of possibilities. These serve as portals to remind us of the inexplicable immediacy of Divine Presence. The genius of this book is not only its vision but also how it calls the reader to take up spiritual practices that open the mind and heart to the radiant light of compassion. Be forewarned—these practices not only console but also call us to stretch beyond our comfort zones, to become larger than ourselves so that we might become who we truly are."
—**Rev. Robert V. Thompson**, author of *A Voluptuous God: A Christian Heretic Speaks*

"Hliboki writes with palpable respect for three of the major faith traditions, identifying common ground but cherishing their distinctiveness. Pastors, retreat leaders or spiritual mentors who value the diversity of religious experience ought to be able to utilize her book as a guide and resource with minimal adaptation for varying circumstances or audiences. Hliboki looks both East and West, and in her book the twain meet."
—**Alexander Patico**, North American Secretary, Orthodox Peace Fellowship

The Breath of God: Thirty-Three Invitations to Embody Holy Wisdom

"*The Breath of God* is a beautiful book, visually and spiritually. As lovely as its artwork is, its rich mix of words and images takes us to the depths of something lovelier still, which many people call God, whose name is both known and unknown. This book moves as the human heart moves, between the seen and the unseen, and somehow embraces it all. Read this book meditatively, in the spirit with which it was written, and it will open your heart—to yourself, to others, and ultimately to the beauty behind this world of suffering and joy."
—**Parker J. Palmer**, author of *On the Brink of Everything: Grace, Gravity, and Getting Old*, *The Courage to Teach*, and *A Hidden Wholeness*

"*The Breath of God*, written and compiled by Julie Hliboki, is a devotional poetic reflection on the most beautiful Names of God, offered through the language of personal experience bringing words together with beautiful artistry creating devotional songs based on the Monotheistic tradition. Dr. Hliboki's poetic reflections bring the reader together with the seeking heart of the wayfarer, a heart that sees beauty in all that exists, experiences divine in every reflection, appreciates the bounty and richness that she has received from the generosity of the Being, yet expressed in a contemporary language for the modern reader."
—**Nahid Angha**, PhD, Co-director of the International Association of Sufism and Executive Director of *Sufism Journal*

"As a teacher of contemplative practice, I am constantly reminded that most practices focus on only one dimension of experience—for example, the use of images rather than words. But Julie Hliboki moves past this narrowness, inviting us into a multi-dimensional contemplative experience. She draws on the wisdom of the Abrahamic spiritual paths to weave together processes of vocal, musical, and visual expression, as well as insights from the sacred words, texts, and sages. By allowing us to activate this full range of contemplative capacities, *The Breath of God* offers us a rare and much-needed experience: a profoundly integrated contemplative practice for the cultivation of a profoundly integrated life."
—**Andrew Dreitcer**, PhD, Associate Professor of Spirituality and Director of the Center for Engaged Compassion, Claremont School of Theology

"A stunning feast of the spirit, this book describes a pathway to God. Through stories of her personal journey, the author shows us how we can breathe God too. By drawing upon faith traditions, she shares wisdom of the ancients. We have been invited on the journey, accompanied every step of the way."
—**Frances Henry**, founder of Global Violence Prevention

Julie Hliboki, DMin, BCC, is passionate about fostering engaged compassion. She has authored six books including *Breathing Light: Accompanying Loss and Grief with Love and Gratitude* and *Cultivating Compassion in and Interfaith World: 99 Meditations to Embrace the Beloved.* Julie also has designed and produced a deck of *Compassion Meditation Cards* for inspiration and prayer.

In the role of a Quaker interfaith chaplain, Julie accompanies people into the richness of life and death. She invites cultivating the sacred, compassionate moments that remind us of our true nature. In addition to Julie's work in healthcare chaplaincy, she accompanies individuals and groups who wish to deepen their experience of the Light. For more information, please visit: *www.JulieHliboki.com.*

CPSIA information can be obtained
at www.ICGtesting.com
Printed in the USA
LVHW070420020422
715112LV00002B/6